U.S. STATES
FLAGS
THE COLORING BOOK

THIS COLORING BOOK BELONGS TO:

_____

_____

B.C. Lester Books
Geography publications for the people since 2019.

Visit us at www.bclesterbooks.com for more!

A MESSAGE FROM THE PUBLISHER

Hey! Thank you for making the purchase, we really hope you enjoy this book. If you have the chance, then all feedback is greatly appreciated. We have put a lot of effort into making this book, so if you are not completely satisfied, please email us at ben@bclesterbooks.com and we will do our best to address the issues. If you have any suggestions, enquries or want to send us a selfie with this book, then email at the same address - ben@bclesterbooks.com

Is this book misprinted? Drop us an email with a photo of the misprint and we will send out another copy!

WHO ARE WE AT B.C. LESTER BOOKS?

B.C. Lester Books is a small publishing firm of three people based in Buckinghamshire, UK. We aim to provide quality works in all things geography, for kids and adults, with varying interests. We have already released a selection of activity, trivia and fact books and are working hard to bring you wider selection. Have a suggestion for us? Then email ben@bclesterbooks.com. We are all ears!

LOOKING FOR A SIMILAR COLORING EXPERIENCE?

Color in some of the most well-known landmarks of the world, from Big Ben to Sydney Opera House!

Take a Safari tour across the famous Serengeti national park and bring it's habitants to life with color.

BEFORE YOU START...

Test your coloring equipment here for bleedthrough. Note that this coloring book is NOT recommended for paint or highlighters...

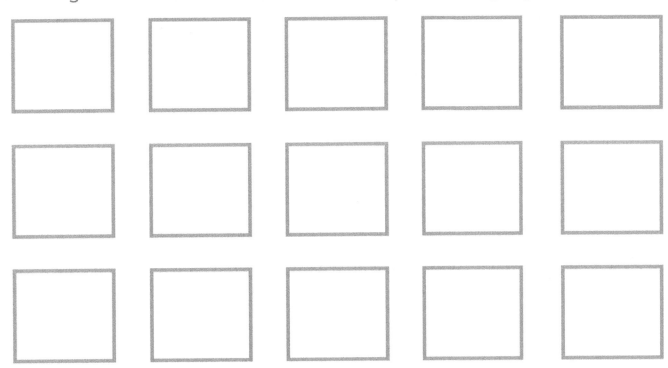

We recommend **coloring pencils** for the flags purely because of the detail on the majority of U.S. state flags, suchas Florida, shown below! Other precise tools such as gel pens may work, but be sure to check the bleedthrough first!

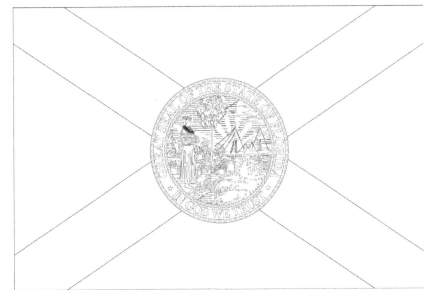

FLORIDA

NUMBERING SYSTEM & RECOMMEND COLORS TO USE

The numbers in a grey square to the right of the name refer to the colors used in the flag. Think of this as more of a hint than a color guide.

FLAG OF WEST VIRGINIA 2 13 16

ACCURACY OF COLORS AND FLAG DETAILS

The flag outlines are mostly exact outlines of the state flag, and any minor changes (such as line thickness) was done purely to improve the coloring experience! The 19 colors suggested at the back are only a guideline and are not the exact colors used within the flag. The 19 colors were picked as a compromise between the availability of those colors and precision to the actual colors of the flag.

B.C. Lester Books

U.S. STATES

AL = Alabama
AK = Alaska
AZ = Arizona
AR = Arkansas
CA = California
CO = Colorado
CT = Connecticut
DE = Delaware
FL = Florida
GA = Georgia
HI = Hawaii
ID = Idaho
IL = Illinois
IN = Indiana
IA = Iowa
KA = Kansas
KY = Kentucky

LA = Louisiana
ME = Maine
MD = Maryland
MA = Massachusetts
MI = Michigan
MN = Minnesota
MS = Mississippi
MO = Missouri
MT = Montana
NE = Nebraska
NV = Nevada
NH = New Hampshire
NJ = New Jersey
NM = New Mexico
NY = New York
NC = North Carolina
ND = North Dakota

OH = Ohio
OK = Oklahoma
OR = Oregon
PA = Pennsylvania
RI = Rhode Island
SC = South Carolina
SD = South Dakota
TN = Tennessee
TX = Texas
UT = Utah
VT = Vermont
VI = Virginia
WA = Washington
WV = West Virginia
WI = Wisconsin
WY = Wyoming
DC = District Of Columbia

DISTRICT OF COLUMBIA

ALABAMA

ALASKA

ARIZONA

ARKANSAS

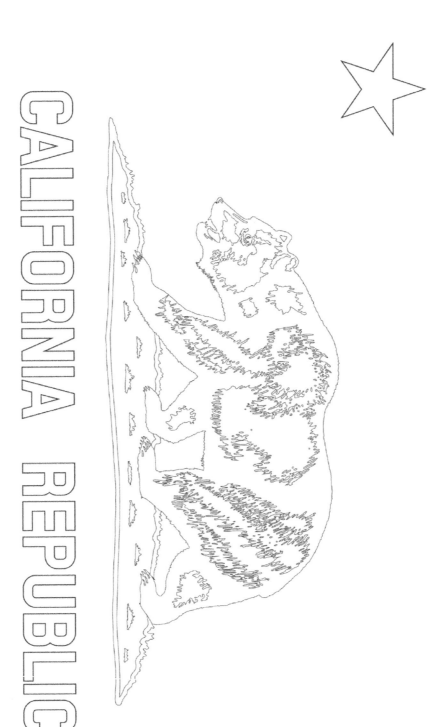

CALIFORNIA

COLORADO

FLAG OF CONNECTICUT

1
5
6
13
16
17

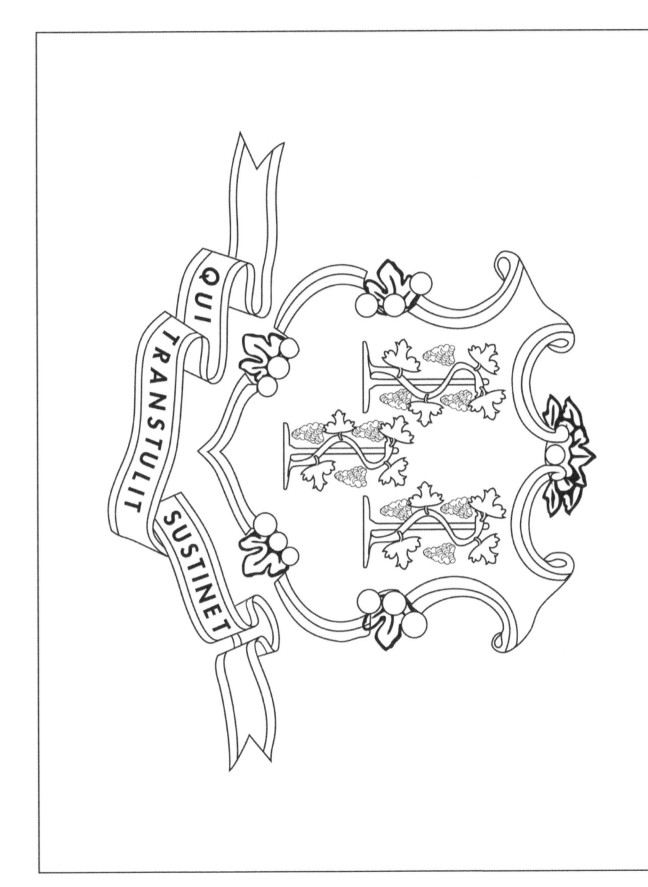

CONNECTICUT

FLAG OF DELAWARE

1
4
5
6
7
9
11
16
18
19

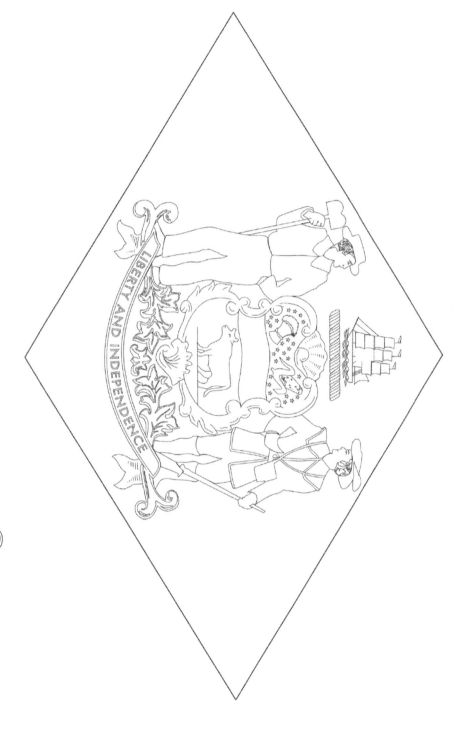

DELAWARE

DECEMBER 7, 1787

FLAG OF FLORIDA

FLORIDA

GEORGIA

HAWAII

FLAG OF IDAHO

STATE OF IDAHO

THE STATE OF IDAHO

GREAT SEAL OF

ESTO PERPETUA

IDAHO

FLAG OF ILLINOIS

ILLINOIS

ILLINOIS

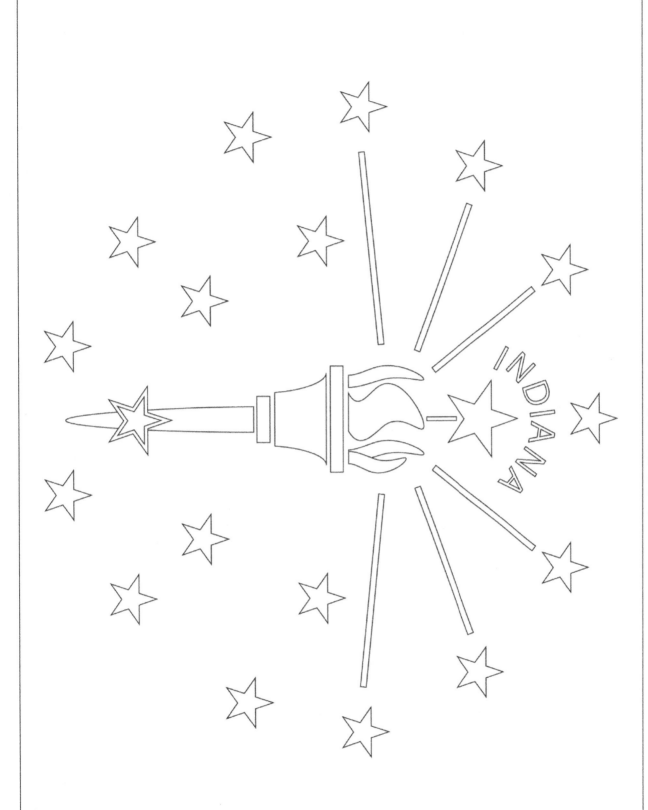

INDIANA

FLAG OF KANSAS

KANSAS

KANSAS

FLAG OF KENTUCKY

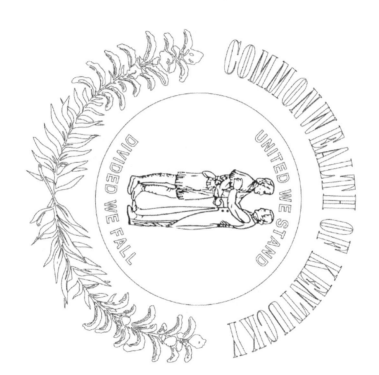

KENTUCKY

FLAG OF LOUISIANA

UNION JUSTICE CONFIDENCE

LOUISIANA

FLAG OF MAINE

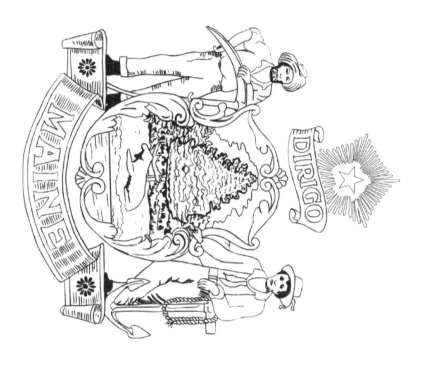

MAINE

MARYLAND

FLAG OF MASSACHUSETTS

MASSACHUSETTS

FLAG OF MICHIGAN

MICHIGAN

FLAG OF MINNESOTA

MINNESOTA

IN GOD WE TRUST

MISSISSIPPI

FLAG OF MISSOURI

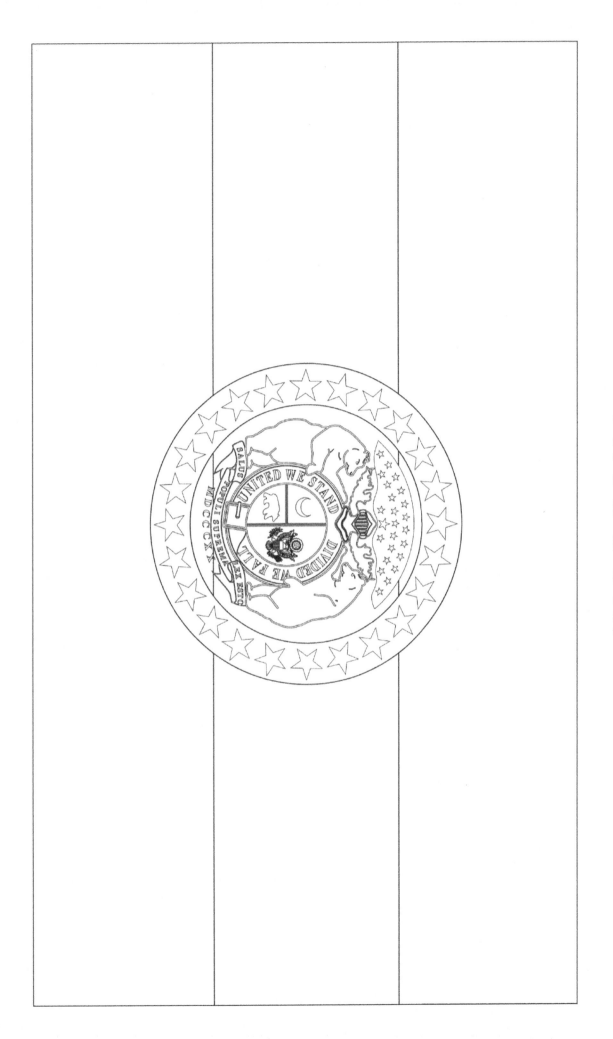

MISSOURI

FLAG OF MONTANA

MONTANA

MONTANA

FLAG OF NEBRASKA

NEBRASKA

NEVADA

FLAG OF NEW HAMPSHIRE

NEW HAMPSHIRE

FLAG OF NEW JERSEY

NEW JERSEY

NEW MEXICO

FLAG OF NEW YORK

NEW YORK

N ☆ C

MAY 20th 1775

APRIL 12th 1776

NORTH CAROLINA

FLAG OF NORTH DAKOTA

NORTH DAKOTA

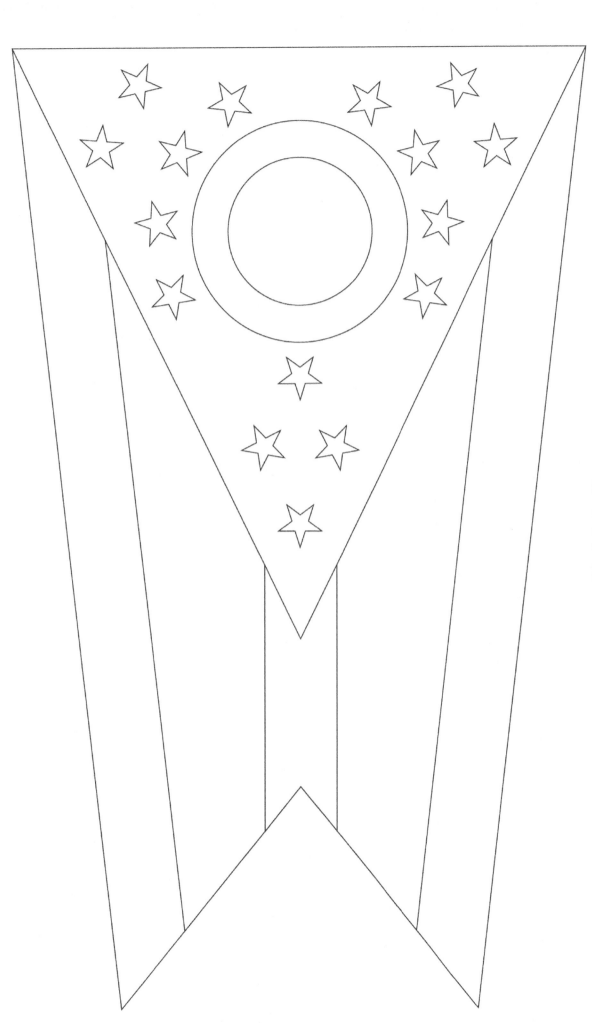

OHIO

FLAG OF OKLAHOMA

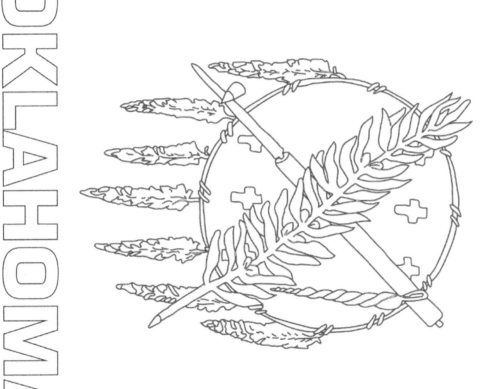

OKLAHOMA

OKLAHOMA

STATE OF OREGON

1859

OREGON

FLAG OF PENNSYLVANIA

PENNSYLVANIA

FLAG OF RHODE ISLAND

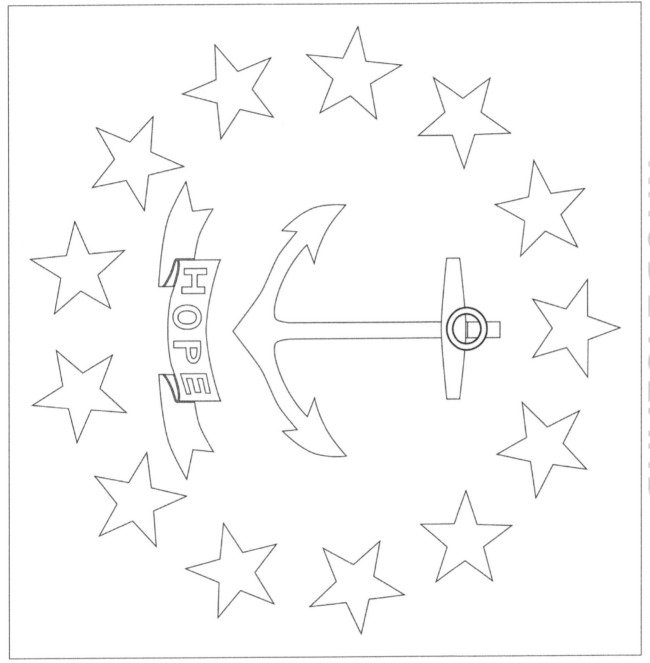

RHODE ISLAND

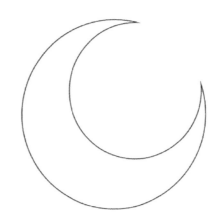

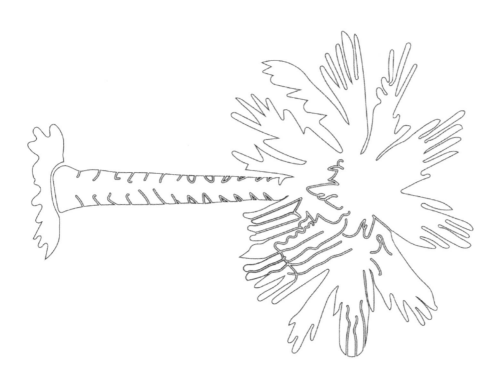

SOUTH CAROLINA

FLAG OF SOUTH DAKOTA

SOUTH DAKOTA

TENNESSEE

TEXAS

UTAH

FLAG OF VERMONT

VERMONT

FLAG OF VIRGINIA

1
2
4
7
10
13
15
16
17
18

VIRGINIA

FLAG OF WASHINGTON

WASAHINGTON

FLAG OF WEST VIRGINIA

WEST VIRGINIA

WISCONSIN

WISCONSIN

FORWARD

1848

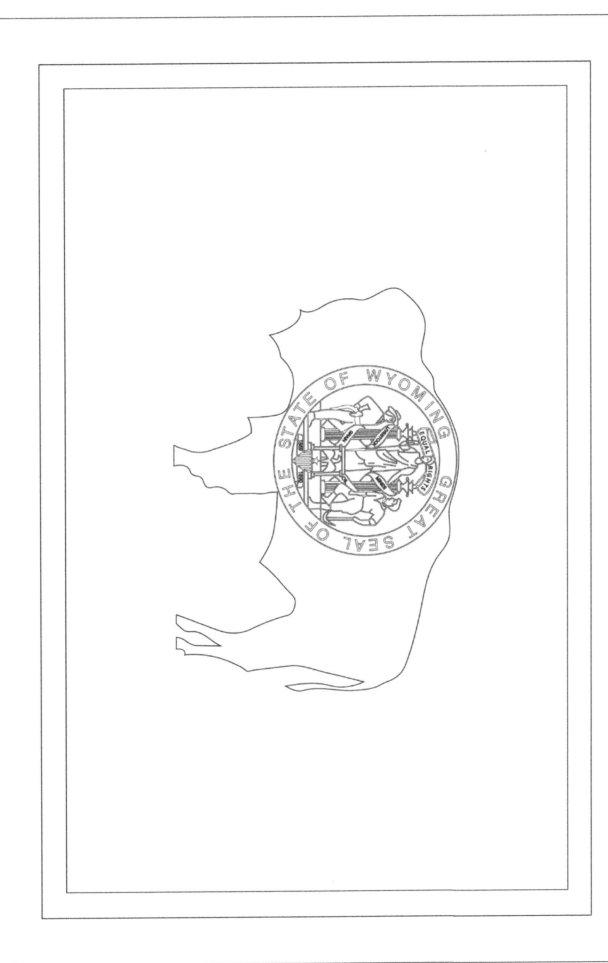

WYOMING

FLAG OF AMERICAN SAMOA

AMERICAN SAMOA

FLAG OF GUAM

GUAM

FLAG OF NORTHERN MARIANA ISLANDS

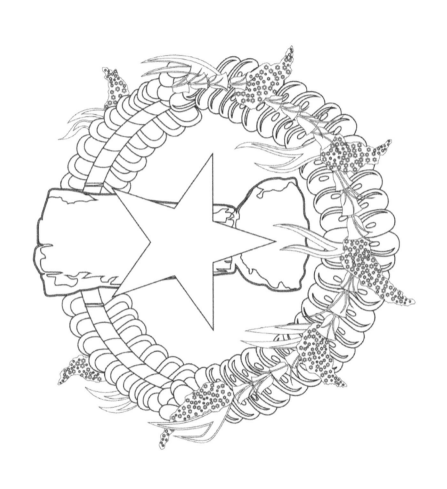

NORTHERN MARIANA ISLANDS

PUERTO RICO

FLAG OF THE U.S. VIRGIN ISLANDS

U.S. VIRGIN ISLANDS

Made in the USA
Las Vegas, NV
21 October 2021